BECOMING

LUCKY

A CAT'S TALE

Joyce McClanahan

Megan Meyer

Dedicated to Dianne and Lucky

Copyright 2023 by Joyce McClanahan   ed.mcclanahan1@hotmail.com
All rights reserved. This book, or parts thereof, may not be reproduced in any form without permission in writing from the publisher.
Summary: A small black cat is hit by a car, rescued and taken home by a lady where he makes friends with the dog and the man who had not wanted him. He grows bigger than the dog and becomes Lucky. The story is presented in black ink drawings and cut out black cats.
ISBN-979-8-218-16437-9

A little black cat scampered across a busy street.

He was almost across when he was hit
by a car. He tried to run but a back leg
did not work.

A lady driving by saw the injured
cat. She parked and hunted but did not find
him. At home she told her husband she
had to look some more. He told her
NOT to bring the cat home.

She went back and hunted
and hunted.
She discovered him curled up
under a bush near the road.

The lady took him to
the doctor who put
a splint and bandage
on his broken leg.

The lucky cat also got shots and a chip telling
that he belonged to the lady.

He loved the lady.

He made friends
with the dog...

...and with the man who had
not wanted him.

He hid
behind a
houseplant.

He hid in the scratching tower.

He hid in
a box.

He was fierce
when teased.

He watched the lady cook from his perch on the kitchen island.

He found food on the kitchen counter.

He grew
BIGGER
than the dog.

He was a very
lucky cat so
his name
became
LUCKY.

THE END

www.ingramcontent.com/pod-product-compliance
Lightning Source LLC
Chambersburg PA
CBHW041037120726
48006CB00006B/1222